I Can Do It:

A Collection of Inspiring Stories About Courage, Respect, Trust and Self-Confidence

Inspired Inner Genius

This book belongs to the wonderful

....

Here at Inspired Inner Genius, we believe that every child is born a genius.

Join us in our journey to inspire the world, one child at a time.

No part of this publication may be reproduced, stored in a retrieval system, or transmitted, in any form, or by any means, electrical, mechanical, photocopying, recording or otherwise without the prior written permission of the publisher or a licence permitting restricted copying.

Written by Jane Alcott · Cover designed by Menna Eissa · Published by Inspired Inner Genius

Free Bonus

Grab the first two eBooks of our flagship Inspired Inner Genius series for free.

Simply visit: https://go.inspiredinnergenius.com/ebook or scan the QR code below to grab two inspirational biography books for your little one(s)!

Table of Contents

Free Bonus .... *v*

Table of Contents .... *vi*

Introduction .... *vii*

1. Home Alone *1*

2. Solo *8*

3. The Sleepover *15*

4. A Doctor's Visit *23*

5. Being Me *30*

6. Thin Ice *37*

7. The Hill *44*

8. Seeing Clearly *52*

9. Lost in the Aisles *59*

10. Summer Camp Choice *66*

Conclusion .... *ix*

Glossary .... *x*

Free Bonus (Reminder) .... *xiii*

Introduction

Special greetings to our precious young reader,

First of all, a very big thank you for picking up this book and giving it a read.

We at Inspired Inner Genius truly believe that the future lies in your young but capable hands.

We believe that you are a remarkable individual who has the power to change the world!

Because of this, we have put together this compilation of stories that we believe will empower you to make an impact on the world, starting from those around you.

This book that you hold in your hands has been written, packaged, and published delicately with abundance of love and care.

In it contains 10 spectacular tales that cover topics ranging from friendship and forgiveness to conquering your fears and decision making. As we dive into each of these stories, we hope that you will be able to relate to the characters and situations. Moreover, we hope that you will draw upon the lessons to apply them to your own lives.

Not only that, but we also hope that you will discover and be reminded that you are brave, thoughtful, and very much capable of conquering anything!

Through this book, we hope to impart to you some of our biggest takeaways that we believe will equip you with the values to make a positive impact on the world.

We sincerely hope that you will enjoy this book as much as we enjoyed creating it specially for YOU.

Well, don't just take our word for it. Dive into the book and find out for yourself!

Without further ado, here are 10 beautiful stories that we hope will touch your heart...

-- The Inspired Inner Genius Team

1. Home Alone

Vivian almost burst with excitement when her parents told her that she got to stay home alone while they went out for a few hours one night. Of course, she wasn't *really* going to be alone; her brother Lucas, who was eight years older than her, was going to be babysitting her. However, Vivian didn't let that fact stop her from grinning with delight as her parents got ready to leave.

No parents—just her and Lucas! They would eat junk food, watch movies, and play outside all night without anyone telling them what to do!

"Remember, honey," said Mom as she gave Vivian a kiss on the cheek, "you need to respect Lucas just like you respect Dad and me. Listen to what he says, okay?"

Vivian nodded. "I will, Mom. I promise."

"I love you!" Mom and Dad sang before they gave Vivian one last wave goodbye.

"I love you too!" Vivian said with a grin and a wave back. As Lucas closed the door behind Mom and Dad, Vivian bounced on her toes. "What are we going to do? Eat ice cream for dinner? Watch a whole TV show? Race down the street with our bikes?"

Lucas chuckled. "Just because Mom and Dad aren't here doesn't mean that we can do anything. We still have to follow the rules, even when they aren't around."

Vivian's heart sank. "But I thought we were going to have fun!"

"We will have fun!" Lucas said. "How about we start out with a game of checkers?"

Checkers was Vivian's favorite game, so she jumped at the chance. "Okay!"

Vivian won the first round of checkers and Lucas won the second. After that, Vivian got bored of the game. "I want to do something else," she said. "Can't we go ride down the street on our bikes?"

"Remember what Mom and Dad always say about going outside at night? It's not safe to ride our bikes when it's dark out."

Vivian crossed her arms and frowned. "But Mom and Dad aren't here!" As she said those words, she remembered that Mom had told her to respect Lucas while they were gone. But he wasn't doing a good job of being in charge—he wouldn't even let her go outside!

"I know it's hard," Lucas said, "but we still have to follow the rules, even when Mom and Dad aren't here. They have those rules in place to protect us. They're letting me watch you tonight because they trust me to take care of you, and I'm not going to let them down."

Vivian could see that he was serious, but she still felt angry that she couldn't do what she wanted. That was when she had a very dangerous idea.

"Can we play hide and seek?" she asked.

"Sure!" Lucas stood up and smiled. "Do you want to hide or count first?"

"I want to hide. I have a really good hiding spot!"

"Okay. I'll count to fifty!" Lucas turned around and covered his eyes. "One...two...three..."

Vivian silently dashed out of the room. Her heart beat so loudly that she wondered if Lucas could hear it. The front door was right in front of her, and she knew her bike was leaning against the side of the house. While Lucas was counting, she could go outside and ride her bike, just like she wanted.

But even as Vivian reached for the door handle, she knew it would be wrong. If Mom and Dad were at home, she wouldn't even dream of going outside when they had told her not to. Mom had told Vivian to respect Lucas, and she had promised that she would listen.

"I can do it," Vivian said. With a sigh, she turned away from the front door.

As Vivian heard Lucas reach twenty-five, she darted into his room and crawled under his bed. She giggled to herself as she pulled his comforter down so that he wouldn't be able to see her underneath. From across the house, she heard him reach fifty.

"Ready or not, here I come!" he called.

Vivian listened carefully. She heard Lucas' footsteps enter her room, but after a minute, he walked back out. He then came into his room and Vivian held her breath. She balled herself up tight even though she knew Lucas couldn't see her.

"Hmm..." Lucas hummed as he searched around the room.

Vivian grinned. She really did have a good spot, and this was so fun, much more fun than riding around outside at night by herself when she couldn't see anything anyway!

Eventually, Lucas wandered off, apparently satisfied that she wasn't in his room. Vivian allowed herself a soft giggle.

Ten minutes passed, and Lucas still couldn't find her! Finally, Vivian heard her big brother say, "I give up, Vivian! You win!"

Gleefully, Vivian crawled out from underneath Lucas' bed and ran to her brother. He looked shocked to see her.

"Where were you?" he exclaimed. "I almost thought you disappeared."

Vivian grinned. "I'm not giving away my perfect hiding spot!"

"Hmph." Lucas frowned and pretended to be mad, but a smile peeked through. "Okay, well, it's my turn to find the perfect hiding spot!"

"Not more perfect than mine!" Vivian laughed and hugged her brother. "Thank you for taking care of me, Lucas. I'm sorry that I didn't want to listen to the rules, but I promise that I'll respect you for the rest of the night—and for the rest of forever."

Lucas hugged her back. "Thank you, Vivian. Now get ready, because I have the best hiding spot in the whole world!"

Moral of the Story:

It can be hard to listen to people who aren't your parents, but when someone is put in charge of you, it's important that you show respect by following their rules and your parents' rules. Vivian almost made a huge mistake by not listening to Lucas, but in the end, she made the right choice and had a fun night playing with him.

2. Solo

Music was Mia's favorite class. She loved to sing at the top of her lungs, and her teacher told her that she was very good at it. Sometimes, the teacher even gave her a solo to sing in front of the class! Mia was shy at the beginning of the year, but now, she knew her whole class and she wasn't afraid to sing in front of them.

Mrs. Rivera, the music teacher, started talking about the end of the year musical that would be performed in front of the whole school. Mia was so excited that her class would be able to sing for everyone. Their families would come too, and Mrs. Rivera said that the whole school auditorium[1] would be full! Mia couldn't even imagine seeing that many people all at once, but she was very excited. The music they were singing was really fun, and she couldn't wait for her parents and her sisters to hear it!

Finally, one day in music class, Mrs. Rivera announced that it was time to assign solos for the musical.

"Remember," she said as she looked over the class, "if you have a solo, you will need to practice very hard. It's fun to be heard in front of everyone, but it will also be more work. At any point in time if you don't want to do your solo anymore, just let me know. Singing a solo is your choice."

That day, Mrs. Rivera told Mia that she had a solo in the second song. Mia gasped. She imagined herself on the auditorium stage in front of all of the people—and it didn't make her feel good! In fact, it made her feel a little queasy[2].

"Wow, Mia!" Mia's friend Rose said to her. "That's amazing! You'll be able to sing in front of the whole school!"

Rose wasn't the only one who was excited for Mia. Many others in her class came up to her and told her how amazing it was that she got such a great solo to sing in front of everyone.

"You got the best solo!"

"It's my favorite part of the whole musical!"

"You're going to sound so good!"

However, the more her classmates encouraged her, the more Mia wanted to tell her teacher she was sick and go home. She didn't tell anyone about her fears except Rose.

"What if I get up there and I forget what to sing?" Mia asked Rose during lunch. "What if I hit a wrong note? What if I sound bad? Then everyone will hear me!"

"But you never sound bad!" Rose said.

"But what if I do this time?"

Rose took a bite of her peanut butter and jelly sandwich and seemed to think very hard about it. "I don't think you'll sound bad," she said eventually.

But that wasn't good enough for Mia.

When she got home that afternoon, Mia didn't want to eat the snack of cheese and crackers that Dad had made for her. Instead, she went straight to her room and sat down on her bed. The more she thought about standing up on the stage and singing, the more she wanted to cry.

"Mia?"

Mia looked up as Dad entered the room carrying the plate of cheese and crackers. "Aren't you hungry?"

Mia frowned. "Not really."

"Did you eat too much for lunch?"

"Maybe."

Dad set the plate down and sat on the bed next to Mia. "You're always hungry when you come home from school. What's wrong?"

Mia wanted to tell her Dad about the solo, but he would just be excited like everyone else, and Mia would still feel afraid. Mia felt tears sting her eyes.

"You know that you can tell me anything, sweetheart," Dad said softly, taking Mia's hand. "I can see that you're upset, and I want to make it better."

Mia sniffed. "No one understands how scary it is," she said.

"What's scary?"

"The solo." She sniffed again and finally looked up at Dad. "Mrs. Rivera gave me a solo in the musical, but I don't want to sing it in front of all of those people. What if I mess up?"

Dad's face stayed very serious. He nodded. "I understand, Mia. Do you know that I still get nervous talking in front of lots of people?"

Mia stared at Dad. "But you're old!"

Dad laughed out loud and grinned. "I may be much older than you, but I still get a little scared every time when I have to present a project at work. But you know what? I present it anyway, and I do a good job."

"How?"

"I practice a lot. I can help you practice, so that way there's no way you can mess up at all!"

Mia smiled, but then frowned again. She still felt scared. "But how do I feel brave enough to do it?"

"You might still be scared when you go sing your solo," Dad said quietly, "but that's okay. You shouldn't let fear stop you from doing the things you love. You are amazing, Mia, and you can do anything."

Mia smiled at her Dad's words. Suddenly, she felt a whole lot better. "Let's go practice right now!"

In a couple of weeks, it was time for the musical. Mia got a little scared when she saw everyone in the audience, but she remembered what her Dad had said and remembered all of the practice she had put in.

"I can do it," she whispered to herself. Then, she stood up and sang.

Mia didn't mess up even once, and afterward, everyone told her that it was the best solo they had ever heard.

Moral of the Story:

Doing things in front of other people can be scary! But just like Mia learned, you have the power to overcome your fears and do the things you love. If you have confidence in yourself, you can do anything!

3. The Sleepover

Jasmine was counting down the days. Only three days until her first ever sleepover! She was so excited that it was all she could ever talk about.

At school, it was all her friends could talk about, too. They sat with one another at lunch, laughing and whispering secrets as they talked about what they were going to do at the sleepover.

"My mom said we can use her nail polish!" Ariana said. The sleepover was going to be at her house, and she claimed that her mom was going to have all the best things ready for the sleepover.

"I've never had my nails painted before!" Jasmine exclaimed. She had seen the older girls at school wearing nail polish, but she'd never really thought about asking for some from her dad.

"That sounds so fun," Isabelle said with a sigh.

Jasmine frowned. "Why do you sound sad? Sleepovers are times to be happy!"

"I don't know if I can go," Isabelle said, barely looking at her two friends. "My mom and dad are both working and my grandma can't drive. There's no one to take me to Ariana's house."

Jasmine beamed. "My dad can take you!"

All of Isabelle's sadness vanished and she beamed a huge smile. "Really?"

"Yeah! I'll ask him tonight!"

"Thank you, Jasmine!" Isabelle hugged her tightly and Jasmine hugged her friend back.

"It wouldn't be a real sleepover without all three of us!"

With that obstacle out of the way, they dove into discussing what kind of food they'd be eating and how late they'd be staying up. However, sadly enough, they were all in different classes, so when lunch was over, they had to part ways.

"See you at recess!" Ariana called. "I'll tell you all about the movies we're going to watch!"

The thoughts filled Jasmine's mind so much that she could hardly focus on school. In fact, by the time school was over, she had already forgotten about asking her dad if Isabelle could ride with them to Ariana's house. She was too busy telling him all of the sleepover details.

"It sounds like you're going to be having a lot of fun," Dad said with a smile in the rearview mirror. "I think it's going to be the perfect first sleepover."

Jasmine thought so too. When she got home, she started packing up her very best pajamas and clothes. She brought her newest stuffed animal and a couple of toys that she wanted to show her friends. She knew that she still had two days to go, but she just couldn't wait!

The next day at school, Jasmine talked with Isabelle and Ariana at lunch again.

"Did you ask your dad if I can ride with you, Jasmine?" Isabelle asked hopefully.

Jasmine realized that she had completely forgotten to ask her dad, but she didn't want to disappoint her friend.

"He said it was fine!" Jasmine lied. She was sure that Dad wouldn't mind picking up someone else, anyway.

The day went smoothly as they created even more plans. The next day, Friday, was the day of the sleepover, and all three girls were bouncing with excitement. Instead of saying goodbye after school, they said, "See you later!"

At home, Jasmine got the rest of her things together in her favorite bag and waited. She tried reading a book, but she couldn't pay attention when the sleepover was only hours away! She thought about getting out some of her toys, but then she saw her toy car, and her toy car reminded her of picking up Isabelle. She had never asked her dad if it was okay!

Jasmine didn't feel so good, even though she was sure her dad wouldn't mind. She walked slowly into the living room with her head down. There, Dad was rushing back and forth to the car with boxes in his arms.

"Dad?" Jasmine asked.

Dad stopped on his way back from the car and wiped his forehead. "Yes, sweetie?"

Jasmine didn't meet his eyes, but instead, twisted her fingers together. "I forgot to ask...can we pick up my friend Isabelle and take her to Ariana's house?"

"What?" Dad asked, his eyes wide. "Your friend asked you today if we could take her?"

Jasmine pressed her lips together. She could lie, but she felt bad enough already. She shook her head. "She asked me two days ago, but I forgot to ask you and then I told her you said it was okay because I knew you wouldn't mind."

Dad straightened up and sighed. "I normally wouldn't mind, but I have to take a lot of boxes to the storage unit and I've already packed everything up carefully in the car beside your seat. We don't have room to pick someone else up!"

Jasmine's eyes filled with tears. "But...we have to bring Isabelle. I told her we would!"

"You should have asked me first, sweetie, and followed through with your promise to your friend. That's called being trustworthy[3]."

Jasmine didn't know what to say. She simply sniffled and cried until her dad knelt down and hugged her.

"I'm sorry, Dad," Jasmine said.

"I forgive you, sweetie, but just remember that when you say you're going to do something, a friend expects you to do it because they trust you. You don't want to throw away that trust, do you?"

Jasmine shook her head.

Dad pulled away and looked Jasmine in the eye. "Another part of being trustworthy is being honest, and I think you need to be honest with your friend about what happened. What do you think?"

Jasmine thought about it. It wouldn't feel good to admit that she lied to Isabelle, but she knew that it was more important to tell the truth.

"I can do it," Jasmine said.

Dad smiled. "Now, we'll be a little late to the sleepover, but if you help me, I think we can unload enough boxes for your friend to fit in the car too."

"Really?" Jasmine gasped. "I'll do everything I can to help!"

In a moment, she was running around and helping her dad get the boxes out of the car. They were a little late in leaving, and they only arrived at Isabelle's house ten minutes after they should have.

Isabelle was so excited when she jumped into the car. "I'm so excited! Thank you for picking me up!"

"You're welcome," Jasmine said, "but there's something I need to tell you. I didn't actually ask my dad about picking you up when I said I would, and we almost didn't get to pick you up because of it! I'm really sorry."

Isabelle continued on smiling. "Thank you for telling me, but it's okay. We're still going to the sleepover, after all, and it's going to be so fun!"

Jasmine felt a huge sense of relief. "You're a good friend, Isabelle."

"And so are you, Jasmine."

They hugged each other, and then the car took off, heading to the best sleepover they would ever have.

Moral of the Story:

When a friend asks you to do something important for them, it means that they trust you. You can show that you're a trustworthy friend by keeping your promises. And if you do make a mistake like Jasmine did, it's okay—but make sure you tell the truth about it! It's important to be a dependable[4] friend.

4. A Doctor's Visit

Ingrid felt sick as she lay in her dark room.

She knew that she didn't have a cold or a fever or a cough. In fact, she really felt okay—except for her stomach. It felt like she had eaten something rotten.

The clock by her bed said 6:05 AM, which meant that it still wasn't time for her to get up yet. But Ingrid was wide awake. She couldn't stop thinking about the place she was going to today. All of the floors, walls, and ceilings were white, all of the people there wore white coats, and it had this particular smell that she hated so much, it made her want to cry.

Today was the day that Ingrid had to go to the doctor's office, her least favorite place in the world.

At 6:30 AM, Ingrid's mom walked into her room and touched her shoulder gently. "Good morning, Ingrid. It's time to get up and eat some breakfast."

Ingrid pulled the covers tighter around her. "I don't want to get up," she said stubbornly.

"But I made such a special breakfast for my brave girl! What will I do with all of the chocolate chip pancakes?"

Ingrid cracked open an eye. "Chocolate chip pancakes?" she asked.

Mom nodded. "They're still warm."

Slowly, Ingrid peeled back her blankets and sat up. "Maybe I can get up for chocolate chip pancakes," she said.

She walked to the kitchen and instantly smelled the warm scent of her favorite breakfast. There was a plate waiting for her at the table with three pancakes stacked on top of each other. Butter and syrup were already spread over the top with a glass of milk on the side.

Suddenly, Ingrid's stomach didn't feel so bad anymore.

After the wonderful breakfast, Mom said it was time to get dressed, and Ingrid's stomach dropped to her toes as she remembered where she was going. She got dressed as slowly as possible until Mom showed up and helped her. Before Ingrid knew it, she was in the car and the house was disappearing behind her. Normally, she liked to watch the fog rise from the road in the morning, but now her own eyes were fogging up with tears.

Mom took Ingrid's hand. "It's going to be okay, Ingrid. I'll be with you the whole time."

Ingrid didn't say anything. There was nothing that could make her feel better.

"Do you know," Mom said, "that I still have to go to the doctor's, and it still makes me scared?"

Ingrid looked at her mom with worry. "I'm going to have to go to the doctor's my whole life?!"

"Doctors make sure that we're healthy. Don't you want to be healthy your whole life?" Mom smiled over at her. "Every time I have to go see the doctor, I wake up and I tell myself, 'I can do it.' Can you do that?"

Ingrid shook her head. Then, to her horror, she saw that they had already arrived at the white building that made her so afraid.

"It's going to be okay, Ingrid. We'll be out of here in no time. I even got us an early appointment so we won't have to wait so long."

Ingrid didn't move. Tears tracked down her face as she crossed her arms.

Mom stopped the car and turned to face Ingrid, rubbing her arm. "Do you remember when you jumped into Aunt Hannah's big pool even though you were scared? I was so proud of you. You're so brave, Ingrid. You can do it."

Ingrid sniffed and looked up at the doctor's office. She knew that no matter what, she would have to go inside eventually. Maybe Mom was right. Maybe she could do it, and even do it without crying. She had gotten through it every time before.

"I can do it," Ingrid whispered.

Mom smiled. "That's right, my brave girl."

They walked into the doctor's office as Ingrid wiped her tears away. They talked to a woman at a counter who grinned at Ingrid and gave her a sparkly sticker. Ingrid smiled as she pasted it on her shirt. Then, the woman led them to a long hallway. The sight of it chilled Ingrid's heart, but she quietly whispered to herself,

"I can do it."

Ingrid and Mom walked to a room where they waited a minute or two for the doctor. When the doctor came in, she was wearing pretty clothes with flowers. Her smile was so big that Ingrid had to smile back.

"Good morning!" she said. "I see you got a sticker—it looks so pretty on you! My name is Dr. Goode, and I'll be making sure you're healthy today. Is that okay?" she asked, looking at Ingrid.

Ingrid nodded.

Dr. Goode was so cheerful that Ingrid realized she wasn't very afraid anymore. The doctor told her that she was very healthy.

"I'm very proud of you for taking such good care of yourself," Dr. Goode said. Ingrid swelled with pride.

But then came the worst part: Dr. Goode announced that Ingrid was due for a shot.

Ingrid felt tears in her eyes again, but Dr. Goode smiled encouragingly.

"I don't like shots either," the doctor sighed, "but it's important to get them because they keep us from getting sick. It's going to feel just like this." She poked Ingrid's arm lightly. "Do you think you can do it?"

Ingrid frowned. How could she do it? It was her least favorite part!

But then she remembered jumping into Aunt Hannah's pool. It felt so good to be brave and discover that she could try something new.

Finally, Ingrid nodded. "I can do it."

Dr. Goode gave Ingrid the shot in her arm. It did sting, and Ingrid did cry a little, but then Dr. Goode and Mom clapped.

"You were so brave!" Mom said, giving Ingrid a hug after it was over.

Dr. Goode put a purple flowery bandage on Ingrid's arm. "You're the bravest little girl I've ever seen!"

Ingrid smiled. The pain had already gone away.

Moral of the Story:

Sometimes, we have to do things we don't want to do, like going to see the doctor. But Ingrid learned that you don't have to be afraid! When you're brave, you may just find that the things that scare you don't seem so scary anymore.

5. Being Me

Gabriela couldn't stop tapping her feet as she waited on the sidewalk for the school bus to arrive.

She looked down at her lunchbox, pink with a huge rainbow across it. Her backpack was also pink, though it was already on her back. Was she *too* pink? What if there was someone who didn't like pink at all? Would they still talk to her? What if the school had a rule that no one was allowed to wear pink?!

"Gabby," Rosa, her older sister, said as she waited patiently beside Gabriela. "It's going to be fine."

Gabriela frowned down at the ground, but normally, she would have smiled. Rosa joked that she could read Gabriela's mind, and right now it really seemed like it.

"But what if people don't like me?" Gabriela asked.

"You'll find people who love you. I promise. You're you, and that's enough." Rosa smiled down at Gabriela. "You're going to have a good day. Just be yourself."

Gabriela nodded as she heard the roar of the bus engine coming around the corner. The bus stopped and a bunch of other kids got on. Gabriela took one last look at Rosa.

Rosa gave her a quick hug, then nudged her forward. "Have a great day! I'll see you later."

Gabriela sighed and got onto the bus last. She stood by the bus driver and looked down the rows of seats. It seemed that all of them were full, and kids were already laughing and chatting with each other.

Gabriela shifted her backpack on her back.

"If you'll please find a seat," the bus driver said kindly, "then we can be on our way."

"Oh. Okay." Gabriela walked forward, hoping a seat would open up. Lots of people stared at her. Many ignored her altogether. There was a seat open toward the middle of the bus, with the other half of the bench occupied by a girl staring out the window silently. Gabriela sat down carefully, trying not to disturb her.

The moment she sat down, the bus took off. Gabriela rattled a little in her seat and looked at the girl next to her. She still hadn't moved.

"Hi," Gabriela said quietly, half-hoping the girl wouldn't hear.

The girl turned so quickly that Gabriela jumped. The girl had dark hair and a red backpack by her feet. Her eyes were bright green.

"Who are you?" the girl asked, looking Gabriela over. Her eyes especially stayed on her backpack and her lunchbox.

Gabriela swallowed. "I- I'm Gabriela. I'm new."

"Well, obviously." She frowned at Gabriela's backpack. "That won't go over well."

"What?" Gabriela asked, feeling a little panicked, like all of her worst nightmares were coming true.

"You'll see." The girl turned back to the window and was silent.

Gabriela clutched her backpack and rode the whole way to school with her heart in her throat. When she arrived, a helpful teacher directed her to her classroom.

And finally, when she got inside, she saw what the girl on the bus meant.

None of the other girls wore a scrap of pink. Red backpacks, red hairbands, red pencils—it seemed that red was the color, and Gabriela hadn't gotten the memo.

Everyone stared at her like she was a pink beacon[5] when she walked into the classroom. Her teacher introduced her, but Gabriela couldn't look anyone in the eye. How could anyone like her now?

The first day at the new school passed, and none of the other girls in Gabriela's class talked to her. She couldn't find the girl on the bus and figured she must be older. Gabriela stayed on her own all day, even during lunch, which was very lonely.

After school, Gabriela couldn't wait to get off the bus. She waited for everyone else to get off so she wouldn't be in their way, and then she hurried outside. She teared up as she saw Rosa waiting for her.

"No one liked me!" she exclaimed, running up to Rosa. "Now I have to get everything in red, and then maybe they'll talk to me and like me."

"What?" Rosa asked. "Slow down. What happened?"

Gabriela told Rosa about how everyone had red things and no one would talk to her.

"Well, did you try saying hi to anyone?"

"Just one person on the bus."

Rosa shook her head and smiled. "I think that's your problem. If you don't try and make friends, people might think you don't want to talk. You should try introducing yourself to all the people in your class tomorrow."

"What? But I don't have any of the right things! All of my stuff is pink!"

"What did I tell you earlier? All you need is yourself. Try tomorrow, and you'll see. They'll love you, pink and all."

The next day, Gabriela sat alone on the bus. She got to her class a little early and remembered what Rosa had told her. She looked at a group of girls talking to each other.

"I can do it," she said softly to herself.

Gabriela put on a smile and walked to the girls. "Hi," she said proudly, "I'm Gabriela and I like pink."

The girls smiled. "Pink is my favorite color too!" one of them said.

"And I like rainbows!" another one chimed in, looking at Gabriela's lunchbox.

And just like that, Gabriela found friends.

Moral of the Story:

It can be hard to be yourself when other people are doing things differently! You may think that you need to do a lot of extra things just to fit in, but remember, just as Gabriela did, that the best thing to be is YOU! Have confidence in yourself, who you are, and what you love. You'll feel happier, and you'll find friends wherever you go.

6. Thin Ice

The chill in the air sent a thrill through Nisha. She loved the cold, but where she lived it was mostly warm all year. That was why the ice skating rink was her favorite place to go!

Nisha and her best friend Ruth giggled as Grandma helped them put on their heavy skates. Once Nisha's feet were snugly inside the skates, she stood up and wobbled. She always had trouble walking around for a few minutes before she got used to tromping[6] across the carpeted floor with her ice skates.

Ruth tripped as she got on her feet, but once Nisha saw that she wasn't hurt, she laughed and helped her friend up.

"Be careful on the rink," Grandma told them. "I'll be right around here if you need anything." She smiled at Nisha and Ruth, and they were off.

On the ice, Nisha immediately glided away from the wall gracefully. Ruth followed immediately after, grinning.

"This is so fun!" she exclaimed.

Nisha just laughed. She loved the feeling of the cold wind rushing in her face as she got faster.

"Hey!" a voice said behind Nisha.

Nisha turned slowly and skid to a stop. A girl with curly red hair and round glasses approached with a smile, stopping abruptly just before Nisha and Ruth. Her skates scraped along the ground and spread ice all over Nisha's legs; Nisha had never seen anyone stop like that with ice skates before.

"You look like you know your way around the ice," the girl said.

Nisha glanced at Ruth. Ruth shrugged, so Nisha spoke. "Um...yeah. We come here a lot."

"I just moved to the area," the girl said quickly, talking almost too fast for Nisha to keep up. "In Michigan where I used to live, there were actual frozen ponds to skate on!"

Nisha didn't know what to say, so she stayed silent. The girl didn't seem to notice as she kept talking. "What kind of skating do you do?"

"We're working on figure skating," Ruth said. "When we're old enough, we're going to join the team."

"Oh, cool! I do hockey." The girl began running in place on the ice—which was impressive, but kind of odd. Nisha bit back a laugh.

"I'm Sam, by the way," the girl said, sticking out a hand. "It's short for Samantha."

Nisha heard Ruth giggle a little beside her. Nisha coughed to cover up her own laugh. This girl was weird! Nisha awkwardly shook her hand and so did Ruth as they said their names.

"It's a pleasure to meet you," Sam said. "I'd like to learn some figure skating techniques; I think it could help with my hockey."

Nisha and Ruth looked at each other. Ruth grinned like she was going to burst out laughing. Nisha fought the same urge and looked away from Ruth quickly.

"Uh...actually, I forgot something back with my grandma and I need Ruth to come with me to get it," Nisha said quickly, pulling Ruth away.

Sam's face fell. "Oh. Well, I'll see you in a little bit, then!"

Nisha and Ruth only just made it off the ice before they both burst into laughter, holding their stomachs.

"That girl was so weird!" Ruth said.

"Did you see her sweater?" Nisha asked. "It looked like my grandpa's!"

The two girls rushed back to Grandma and quickly told her about what had happened with Sam. Grandma, however, didn't seem to find it funny. "You didn't tell her that you thought she was weird, did you?"

"No!" Nisha said. "I know that's rude."

Grandma didn't look impressed as she crossed her arms. "It's also rude to talk about someone behind their back."

Nisha looked down, feeling guilty.

"But you should have seen her," Ruth said. "Then, you would understand."

"I don't need to see her," Grandma said. Nisha met her eyes. "All I know is that everyone deserves respect, no matter how different they look or act from you." Grandma smiled. "You probably look and act much different from her, but she was friendly enough to introduce herself."

All at once, Nisha knew that her grandma was right.

"So," Grandma continued, "what do you think you should do now?"

"We can't talk to her," Nisha said. "She makes us laugh at her."

"You *can* talk to her," Grandma said. "Do you think you can show her respect by not laughing at her or calling her weird?"

Ruth looked at Nisha. Nisha wasn't sure what to say. It seemed impossible when that girl was so odd! But at the same time...her hair looked a little like one of Nisha's favorite TV show characters. Maybe she could think about that.

"I can do it," Nisha said with a nod, looking at her grandma. "Come on, Ruth." Nisha turned and headed back to the ice. Sam was easy to spot with her red hair and Nisha immediately went toward her.

"I don't know if I can stop laughing," Ruth whispered.

"Yes you can!" Nisha whispered back. "Just try."

Finally, they reached Sam. "Hi!" Nisha said.

When Sam turned around, Nisha found it easy not to laugh. Actually, on another look, she thought that Sam's sweater looked really cozy—and cool.

"Hey, you're back!"

Nisha smiled. "How about this: we'll teach you some figure skating if you teach us some hockey."

Ruth beamed. "That sounds so fun!"

Sam smiled too, with excitement in her eyes. "Deal!"

And Nisha had more fun that day at the skating rink than she ever had before.

Moral of the Story:

Everyone is different. Some people may seem like they're exact opposites of you, but they still deserve your respect just like anyone else! Be like Nisha and show kindness and respect to those who may be different from you. You may just find a new friend!

7. The Hill

"Mom, can you come with me while I ride on my scooter?"

Mom smiled down at Kaylani, but Kaylani saw the sad look in her eyes. she knew the answer would be no before Mom even opened her mouth.

"I'm sorry, sweetie, but I have some calls to make for work tonight, and Luke is still at the office."

Kaylani winced[7]. She still didn't like Luke, even though he was supposed to be her new dad. He was really nice to her, but she didn't trust him or his son Jayden.

"But I want to go outside," Kaylani said. She knew that she wasn't allowed to go out without a grownup, since they lived in an apartment complex and didn't have their own backyard.

"You can ask your brother," Mom said. "I'm sure he'd love to do that with you."

Kaylani looked down. Why would she ask Jayden to go with her? She didn't like him any more than she liked Luke.

Mom touched Kaylani's chin. Kaylani looked into her mother's soft eyes.

"I know that everything is a little different, honey, but this is the way things are now. You should get to know Jayden. He really is a nice boy. I think you two would be good friends if you talked to each other."

"Then why doesn't he ever talk to me?" Kaylani asked.

Mom's eyes lit up. "Do you know what? He's shy. I think he's worried that you don't like him."

Kaylani thought of Jayden, tall and lanky[8]; he was in middle school, which meant that he was *way* older than her! And he was afraid of her?

She giggled and Mom joined in. "See? You should let him know that he doesn't have to be afraid of you."

Kaylani frowned and thought some more. She really did want to go outside, and it seemed that Jayden was the only way she'd be able to do that.

"Okay."

She went to the back of the apartment where Jayden's room was and stared at the door. It suddenly looked huge, and Kaylani wondered if staying inside wouldn't be so bad.

No. It was such a nice day outside; she just had to ride her scooter! She knocked on Jayden's door lightly and waited.

In a moment, Jayden opened the door. "Yeah?" He frowned, looking confused as he saw Kaylani.

"Um…" Now Kaylani was the one who felt afraid of him. "Will you go outside with me? I want to ride on my scooter but there's no one else to watch me."

Jayden glanced over his shoulder. His computer screen was lit up and he seemed to be in the middle of some sort of game. His eyebrows mashed together and he seemed to be thinking really hard.

"Okay," he said finally. "Just give me a minute to put my shoes on."

"Yay!" Kaylani exclaimed.

A small smile touched Jayden's lips. He turned around, leaving his door open. Kaylani skipped to her room and put her own shoes on.

"Mom, Jayden and I are going outside!" she called.

Mom appeared from the kitchen with a grin. "That's great, honey! Be careful!"

"I will!"

Jayden didn't have his own scooter, but he carried Kaylani's for her as they walked downstairs to the bottom of the complex. Once they reached the sidewalk, he placed her scooter facing town, the way that Kaylani always rode when Mom was with her.

"Let's go the other way," Kaylani said, turning her scooter the other way after she strapped on her helmet.

Jayden frowned and crossed his arms. "We should go toward town. Isn't that the way you usually go?"

"Yes, but I want to go a new way."

"Your mom takes you the normal way for a reason. Going toward town is much safer. This way has a lot of hills that are hard to ride with a scooter."

"Well, you can go that way. I'm going this way, just for a few minutes." Kaylani kicked her foot out and started gaining speed down the opposite way she usually went.

Jayden's footsteps caught up to her. "Wait!"

Kaylani laughed as she saw him stumbling after her. She pedaled faster and then looked back and grinned at Jayden as he fell behind her.

"Kaylani! Look out!" Jayden called.

Kaylani looked ahead. Suddenly, the sidewalk turned into a sharp slope and she was racing downward. The ground blurred underneath her. What could she do? She was going too fast!

Suddenly, Kaylani stopped and came to an instant halt. In front of her was Jayden, huffing and puffing, sweat running down his forehead. He had his foot wedged in front of the wheel and his hands on the handlebars.

Tears came into Kaylani's eyes as her fear caught up with her. She also felt shame, as Jayden had told her this way was unsafe.

"I'm sorry," she sniffed, unable to look at Jayden's face. "I should have trusted you."

Jayden finally relaxed, though he still held the scooter firmly in place. "I'm just glad you're okay." He sighed. "I know that you haven't known me for very long, but haven't I proved that I'm trustworthy?"

Kaylani thought about the times he'd walked her to school, the one time he'd protected her from a bully, the way he always told her the truth. She hung her head.

"I know it can be hard to trust new people," Jayden said, "but if their actions prove that you can trust them, it's a good thing to have someone else on your side. So, will you trust me to lead you in the right direction?"

Kaylani looked up into Jayden's eyes. She still didn't want to like or trust him; he and his dad had interrupted the good, quiet life she'd had with Mom.

But he had just saved her, and he had proved his trustworthiness time and time again.

"I can do it," Kaylani said with a nod. "I do trust you, and I'll try to be trustworthy myself from now on."

Jayden smiled. "Well, this is a good start."

Together, they turned and raced in the opposite direction toward town.

Moral of the Story:

When Kaylani failed to trust Jayden, even after he proved himself to be trustworthy, she put herself in danger. Don't let prejudice—deciding not to like someone for no reason—get in the way of trust! It's important that we have good people to depend on so that they can help us and steer us in the right direction.

8. Seeing Clearly

Felicity squinted⁹ at the board in front of the classroom. She was supposed to copy down the math problem that Mrs. Carrow had written up there, but she couldn't quite see some of the numbers. Was that a two, or a five? Having a headache didn't make things any easier.

"Felicity?" Mrs. Carrow asked. "Do you have an answer for the equation yet?"

"Not yet, Mrs. Carrow," Felicity said, relaxing her eyes. She didn't want to look at her teacher. Felicity had been given plenty of time to figure out the math problem, but what could she do if she couldn't even see the numbers on the board?

"That's okay, keep working it out and talk to your partner if you need help."

Felicity glanced over at her partner, Austin, whose desk was next to hers. He was very quiet, and he seemed nice, but she still felt afraid to talk to him. What if he asked why she needed help?

Before Felicity could make up her mind, Austin tilted his paper toward her. "Here you go," he whispered.

Felicity sighed with relief and offered Austin a smile. He smiled back as she copied just the problem, not the answer, that was on his paper.

Austin pushed his glasses further up on his nose and Felicity flinched. If she wore her glasses like she was supposed to, she would likely be able to see the board just fine. However, she had seen how some of her classmates had made fun of Austin for his glasses. They said that his eyes didn't work right and called him an old man. Austin didn't seem to mind, but it hurt Felicity. She thought about what she would feel like if people said those things to her.

Felicity solved the math problem, but by the time she worked it out, someone else had already answered it for Mrs. Carrow. Felicity sighed. Mrs. Carrow probably thought she hadn't been paying attention. She loved her teacher, and she didn't want her to think that she wasn't doing her best. Felicity always did well in school—until recently, when she couldn't read the board.

After math class, it was time to pack up for lunch. They were allowed to "chatter," which meant that they could talk quietly as long as they were still cleaning up.

"My glasses help me a lot," Austin said quietly beside Felicity.

Felicity glanced over at him, surprised that he was finally talking to her.

"I can see that it's hard for you to read the board," he continued, looking down at his desk. "Maybe you can ask your parents to get you some glasses. It makes me feel so much better and I don't have headaches anymore."

Felicity gasped. Could she be having a headache because she wasn't wearing her glasses?

"I already have a pair of glasses," Felicity whispered so that no one but Austin could hear. "I don't want to wear them."

Austin frowned. "Oh." He seemed to think really hard for a few seconds before he looked back at Felicity. "My dad says that you don't have to let other people make you feel bad for how you look or what you wear. No one else can control who you are but you." He grinned. "And I bet your glasses look really cool."

"I like yours," Felicity admitted. They were red and had cars racing across the frames. She loved cars, but that was something else that no one at school knew about her. They would think a girl who liked cars was weird.

"Felicity?"

Felicity heard Mrs. Carrow call her name and felt very cold. Would she have to tell Mrs. Carrow about her glasses too?

Felicity said goodbye to Austin and walked up to the teacher's desk as everyone else lined up for lunch.

"Felicity," Mrs. Carrow said softly, "I've been noticing for the past few weeks that you haven't been on top of things like usual. I saw you squinting at the board today; I thought your parents got you some glasses."

Felicity fidgeted. "They did, but I don't want to wear them. I look funny in them, and everyone makes fun of Austin for his glasses."

Mrs. Carrow frowned. "When was the last time you saw someone making fun of Austin?"

Felicity thought about it and couldn't remember. "A long time ago," she admitted.

Mrs. Carrow smiled kindly. "A few people said they didn't like Austin's glasses at first, but no one says anything about them now. And most of the class liked them from the start. I certainly do! There's nothing wrong with you or your glasses, Felicity. You simply need an extra, stylish tool right now that many of your classmates will probably need eventually, too."

"Stylish…" Felicity murmured[10].

When she went home that day, Felicity put her glasses on in her room and looked at herself in the mirror. Her glasses were purple and had a pink streak running through them. Now that she thought about it, they *did* look pretty cool.

The next morning, Felicity got out of her dad's car as he dropped her off at school. She hesitated before getting out of the car.

"I can do it," she said, holding her head up high.

Felicity walked into school that day with her glasses on. Most people said nothing, but a few people actually complimented her glasses.

As Felicity walked into her classroom, Mrs. Carrow smiled at her. Austin did too. A few of her classmates whispered as they looked at her, but she didn't mind them as she sat at her desk.

Austin turned to face her. "You look fantastic."

Felicity smiled. She thought she did, too.

Moral of the Story:

It's not bad to look different from other people! Everyone is unique. Some people wear glasses, like Felicity and Austin, some people have different colored skin, and some people may need to use wheelchairs or other special tools. No matter how you look or what you wear, you can hold your head high because you are the most wonderful thing you can be: you!

9. Lost in the Aisles

Carmen skipped behind Mom as they walked into a special grocery store. It was Carmen's favorite because it was ten times as big as a normal grocery store! Mom didn't always let her come to the special grocery store, but today, Mom had told Carmen that she could pick out one thing she wanted as they shopped for groceries. During the whole ride to the store, Carmen had been imagining what she would pick out.

"Remember, Carmen," Mom said as she took a cart and walked into the huge building. "Stay by my side at all times. If you can't find me, go straight to an employee behind a counter and tell them you need to find me. They wear red jackets with blue buttons. They'll know what to do."

Carmen nodded, but her mind was already wandering as she gazed at the ceiling so high above her. How many different things fit inside this huge store?!

First, they passed the deli area. A nice lady let Carmen try a piece of cheese—cheese was her favorite! It was so good that Carmen immediately knew that was what she wanted to get.

"But we've barely even started!" Mom said. "What if you find something else you want later? We can always come back for the cheese."

"Okay," Carmen sighed, but she was sure that she wouldn't find anything more wonderful than that cheese.

Next, they walked around where the bread and crackers were. While Mom was trying to figure out which bread to buy, Carmen spied a huge box of her favorite cheese crackers—and they were in special shapes! She ran off to get a better look. They looked so good! Maybe she wanted these instead of the cheese. She would love to take the special crackers to school and show them to her friends.

Carmen reached up onto her toes and grabbed the giant box. She had to hold it in both arms, it was so big! She turned around to show it to Mom...

But Mom wasn't there!

Carmen froze. Where had she gone? She had just been there looking at the bread. Maybe she would be in the next aisle. But Carmen looked in the next aisle and didn't see her.

Carmen's heart started to beat very fast. She was lost!

Suddenly, the cheese crackers didn't seem so important. In her search for Mom, one of the grocery store employees saw her. A button on his jacket said his name was Daniel.

"Hi there," Daniel said with a kind smile, "are you lost? Do you need any help?"

Carmen looked into his eyes and didn't know what to do. How could she admit that she had run away from her mom for some crackers? And even if she could, how could she talk to someone she didn't know?

"I'm okay," she mumbled, and walked in the other direction. She could find Mom on her own anyway, couldn't she? Talking to grown-ups was too hard.

But the more she searched, the more lost she became. She didn't even know where the bread aisle was anymore, and somehow she had found her way into the cold seafood section.

Carmen shivered. What could she do?

Across the aisle, Carmen saw an employee behind a counter that displayed all different kinds of fish to eat. Mom had said that an employee would know what to do if Carmen got lost, but how could she talk to them? Daniel was nice, but how would she know what to say? What if they thought she was silly or didn't believe her?

Carmen sighed. If she wanted to find Mom, she would have to be brave.

"I can do it," she said.

Still hugging the box of crackers, Carmen marched up to the counter.

"Excuse me?" she asked, her voice sounding much more confident than she thought it would.

The employee looked down at Carmen. She was very pretty, and her eyes were very kind. Her blue button said her name was Lou.

"Hi," Lou said. "How can I help you?"

Carmen felt embarrassed and scared, but it helped that the woman smiled. "I'm lost," she said in a whisper, not looking into the woman's eyes. "I walked away from my mom to get these." She held out the crackers.

Lou walked out from behind the counter and crouched to meet Carmen's eyes. "You must be very brave. I don't think I would be so calm if I were lost. What's your name?"

"Carmen." She smiled, already feeling a little better.

"I can get you back to your mom," Lou said. "Do you know her name?"

"Alexandra."

Lou grinned. "And you're very smart, too! You did the right thing in coming to me. Let's go to the front of the store so we can find your mom."

Lou took Carmen to the front of the store, and there, at another counter, was Mom!

"Carmen!" Mom exclaimed. "I'm so glad you're here! I was so worried!"

"She was very brave," Lou said. "She came right up to me and told me that she needed help."

Mom smiled and hugged Carmen. "That's my strong girl."

Carmen had felt so lost and afraid a few minutes ago, but now she felt confident and sure. Mom held out her hand and Carmen took it.

"Let's finish up our shopping trip," Mom said.

Carmen turned and handed the crackers back to Lou. "Here you go. I don't need them anymore. And thank you for helping me."

"You're very welcome, Carmen. It was nice to meet you!"

"It was nice to meet you, too, Lou!"

At the end of the trip, Mom got Carmen that special cheese, and they ate it with their lunch back home. By the time they sat down to dinner, Carmen forgot she had ever gotten lost at all.

Moral of the Story:

Getting lost can be a very scary thing, but most of the time, the people looking after you are closer than you realize! Carmen could have just sat down and cried, but instead, she decided that she had the courage to talk to one of the employees and ask for help. If you find yourself in trouble, it's always a good idea to ask for help from someone in authority like a parent, an employee, or a teacher. Having courage will help you get through scary situations!

10. Summer Camp Choice

"Time to get up! We've got a fun day planned ahead!"

April shot up out of bed and immediately jumped to her feet. Summer camp was always full of fun activities that April hardly wanted to sleep at all, so waking up wasn't a problem. Some of the other girls in her cabin groaned, as it was still very early in the morning, but April smiled as she saw the sun rising up in the sky.

April's leaders led her and the rest of Cabin 3 to breakfast in a big cafeteria. As soon as they stepped inside, April could smell countless good things to eat. She ate her fill of pancakes, fruit, and eggs, sitting at a table with some of her new friends: Eleanor, Audrey, and Margaret.

Eleanor was just taking a sip of her orange juice across from April when someone stumbled into Eleanor. She spilled her juice all over her lap and gasped, looking down at her wet clothes. The person who had bumped into her walked by and laughed. She was a tall girl with beautiful clothes, and she even wore makeup! April was so distracted by the girl's perfect appearance that she forgot about what had happened to her friend.

"That was so mean!" said Audrey, who was piling napkins into Eleanor's lap.

"Yeah," April said. "Who *was* that?"

"Kinsley Meadows," Margaret sighed. "She thinks she's perfect."

Eleanor met April's eyes. "Can you get one of our leaders so she can take me back to our cabin? I need to change."

"Sure!" April jumped up, eager to help.

After Eleanor changed into dry clothes back at the cabin and the day moved on, April forgot about the event at breakfast until that afternoon. It was one of her favorite times of the day because they had free time where they could pick whatever activity they wanted to do.

One of the activities was archery, where they got to shoot suction arrows at targets. It made April's arms sore, but she loved it anyway. It made her feel just like a hero in a book! So, of course, she picked archery for her free time activity, and Margaret came with her.

"Look how fast I can do it!" April said, letting an arrow go. It missed the target and she and Margaret both laughed.

"I can do it better!" Margaret tried, but her arrow missed the target too, and they both dissolved into giggles.

On April's other side, Kinsley Meadows was hitting the target almost every time. After a little while, she put her bow down and sighed.

"I'm hungry," she said. She looked over at April. "Aren't you?"

April shrugged. Her stomach grumbled; she was always hungry. "I guess so, but dinner isn't for a little while."

Kinsley waved her hand. "That's okay, I can get snacks whenever I want. Want to come with me?"

"Sure!"

Margaret pulled April away. "April, Kinsley likes to break the rules. You shouldn't go with her."

"But she's offering me food. That's nice, isn't it?" April thought that Kinsley running into Eleanor earlier *wasn't* very nice, but maybe it was just an accident.

"We need to go now if you're coming," Kinsley said.

April listened to her stomach. She really wanted food. "Okay, I'll come."

Kinsley told April to wait while she talked to the nearest leader. When she came back, she smiled. "We can go!"

"The leader said so?" Margaret asked. "Who's going to walk with you?"

"No one. I'm allowed to go by myself because I'm older."

That made April uncomfortable. At the start of summer camp, all of the campers had been told that they couldn't go anywhere without an adult.

"That's against the rules," April said.

Kinsley shrugged. "You can think what you want, but I'm going to get some food. Are you coming or not?"

April looked between Margaret and Kinsley. Who did she trust? April was hungry, and Kinsley knew how to get food, but something was wrong. The leader wouldn't let them go on their own. Plus, Kinsley *had* laughed after bumping into Eleanor earlier, and Margaret had been the one helping Eleanor.

But April was *so* hungry, and Kinsley didn't look like she was trying to trick April. She had such nice clothes and hair; couldn't April trust her? But Margaret always followed the rules and was nice to everyone. It was a hard choice, April knew what she had to do.

I can do it, April thought.

"Sorry," she said to Kinsley, "but I trust my friend."

"Whatever." Kinsley walked off by herself. April felt a little bit of regret, but once she and Margaret picked up their bows and arrows, she forgot that she was hungry.

Later that day, April heard some girls in her cabin talking about how Kinsley got in big trouble for sneaking into the kitchen and stealing food when she wasn't supposed to. April realized that had almost been her.

"I'm sorry I didn't listen to you at first," April said to Margaret as they were getting ready for bed that night. "Thank you for being a good friend."

Margaret smiled. "It's okay. You're a good friend too, April, and I'm glad that you trusted me."

Moral of the Story:

Sometimes, it can be hard to know who to trust. April had trouble deciding whether she should listen to her friend Margaret or Kinsley, a girl she didn't know very well. If you look at someone's actions, they will likely show how trustworthy they are. If they have been mean and rude to people, like Kinsley, you probably shouldn't trust them until they show some true acts of kindness. But you can trust the people who have been kind and loyal to you in the past, like your friends! When in doubt, you can always talk to an adult about it.

Conclusion

Even though we've come to the end of the book, know that growing as a person does not stop here.

Just like the characters in each of the stories, know that growing and learning is a continuous and ongoing process!

As long as we have the strength to admit our mistakes, the courage to try again, and the boldness to take a chance, anything is possible.

We hope that you've been inspired by these beautiful stories. Hopefully, they've made a difference in the way you view things and people around you too.

Regardless of whatever comes your way, just remember to tell yourself:

I Can Do It!

Glossary

1 Auditorium
A part of a theater or concert hall which audience sits in

2 Queasy
Feeling Sick

3 Trustworthy
Able to be relied on as honest or trustful

4 Dependable
Reliable or trustworthy

5 Beacon
Light set up in high or prominent position as a signal or celebration

x

Tromping
6 Walk heavily

Winced
7 A slight involuntary shrinking movement of the body out of pain

Lanky
8 Used to describe a person that is thin and tall

Squinted
9 In attempt to see more clearly with one or both eyes partly closed

Murmured
10 Say something in a low, soft or indistinct voice

Free Bonus (Reminder)

Don't forget to grab the first two eBooks of our flagship Inspired Inner Genius series for free!

Simply visit: https://go.inspiredinnergenius.com/ebook or scan the QR code below to grab two inspirational biography books for your little one(s). You'll love them!

Printed in Great Britain
by Amazon

83512934R00051